Where's Baby Jesus?

Illustrated by:
Ashley Boh

Kimberlee
Eckman

WestBow Press books may be ordered through booksellers or by contacting:

WestBow Press
A Division of Thomas Nelson & Zondervan
1663 Liberty Drive
Bloomington, IN 47403
www.westbowpress.com
844-714-3454

Interior Image Credit: Ashley Boh

ISBN: 978-1-6642-8275-9 (sc)
ISBN: 978-1-6642-8276-6 (e)

Library of Congress Control Number: 2022920221

Print information available on the last page.

WestBow Press rev. date: 10/31/2022

WESTBOW
PRESS®
A DIVISION OF THOMAS NELSON
& ZONDERVAN

In loving memory of
Miss Mei-Mei Olive Elisabeth Jacqueline Russell Eckman
&
Pearl

I want to dedicate this book to my grandchildren –
Finn, Lyla, Bennett, and Ezra.

Mama set the groceries, the ingredients for baking Christmas cookies, on the kitchen counter.

She walked through the dining room to hang up her coat and glanced over at the nativity figures arranged on the buffet . . .

. . . and saw that baby Jesus was not lying in the manger. "Where's baby Jesus? Someone has taken baby Jesus!"

Mama looked under the buffet.

She surveyed the living room.

Then she checked on top of the cupboard,

6

behind the sofa,

and under the chair.

She called upstairs to her son. "Have you seen baby Jesus? Baby Jesus is missing." He didn't hear. He was playing the guitar.

9

So, she walked upstairs . . .

. . . and looked around the bedroom,

under the bed,

and under the dresser.
"Where's baby Jesus?
Where can he be?"

Mama walked back downstairs . . .

. . . and back to the buffet. She knelt down and
reached far back. Did she feel something?

16

"I think I know who took baby Jesus," she announced.

17

Do you?

Mei - Mei

Pearl

18

The nativity figurines in this story come from the Provence region of France. They are called santons which translates to little saints. The figurines are made of terracotta. They represent the colorful Provençal people, their traditional trades, activities, and costumes. The santons carry their humble, local offerings to the manger where Jesus was born.

Printed in the United States
by Baker & Taylor Publisher Services